RAITH ROVERS
FOOTBALL CLUB
1991/92–1995/96

Raith Rovers' first ever competitive European match took place on a very sunny evening on Tuesday 8 August 1995. Gotu Itrottarfelag from the Faeroe Islands were Raith's opponents and the home side ran out winners 4-0.

RAITH ROVERS FOOTBALL CLUB
1991/92–1995/96

TONY FIMISTER

First published in 2002

Reprinted in 2014 by
The History Press
The Mill, Brimscombe Port,
Stroud, Gloucestershire, GL5 2QG
www.thehistorypress.co.uk

Copyright © Tony Fimister, 2002, 2014

ISBN 978 0 7524 2425 5

Printed in Great Britain.

Rangers' Gary Stevens and Raith's Jason Dair in action during the 1993/94 league campaign.

Contents

Introduction		7
Acknowledgements		8
1.	Early Days	9
2.	A Dream Start	17
3.	The Path to Glory	37
4.	The 'Windae Hingers'	51
5.	Too Many Draws	69
6.	Blue Cans of Coke	77
7.	Would a Captain Miss?	89
8.	Make Mine a Double	97
9.	A European Goal	105
10.	Goodbye Jimmy	121

Raith's Coca-Cola Cup final hero, goalkeeper Scott Thomson.

Introduction

I have been a fan of Raith Rovers FC since my primary school days. Living only a mile from the ground, I can remember hearing the cheers of the huge crowds that used to turn up for matches back in the mid-1950s. During the 1962/63 season, I started to go to every home game; soon, I was a season ticket holder, and had started to go to all the away games with the supporters club. I have been hooked ever since, and have missed only four home games since 1972.

Apart from the fortunes of Raith, my other main hobby has been photography. One day during the summer of 1991 I decided to pay a visit to Starks Park with the intention of purchasing my season ticket, a trip that I had regularly made over the previous twenty-nine years. This visit to the club's office was to be slightly different, in that I decided to take along a camera in the hope that I would be allowed to take some photographs of the stadium. Susan Rankin, the office secretary, duly issued my season ticket and happily agreed to my request to fire off a few frames around the ground. Like most stadiums during the closed season, Starks Park was immaculate. A lick of paint here and there, some new advertising boards and a pitch, prepared by groundsman Andy Leigh, that looked like a championship snooker table. Afterwards, I returned to the office, thanked Susan for her co-operation and left clutching my newly printed fixture list.

About a week after this visit to the stadium, I received a phone call from Susan Rankin asking me if I would like to take over the position of club photographer from Bob Mackie, who was about to join the local newspaper and wouldn't be able to combine both jobs. Although I did ask for some time to be able to consider her offer, my mind was made up straightaway – the opportunity to combine both my hobbies and be of service to my club was too good to miss.

Raith Rovers chairman Peter Campsie explained the club photographer's duties to me. I was to report to the ground at least thirty minutes before kick-off, take a photograph of the match sponsor and their guests on the pitch, plus a shot of the mascot with his or her favourite player, and any other photographic requests of the commercial department, then it was off to my seat in the stand to watch the game. When the match was over, I was to report to the sponsors' lounge, take a photograph of the match sponsor presenting a gift to the man of the match and finally a photograph of the ball sponsor being presented with a signed football. I was so proud to be a part of the club that I had supported since I was twelve years old.

Of course, no one knew the change in fortunes that was about to occur at Raith Rovers over the next few seasons. From being an average, middle of the table First Division club, Raith were about to experience the most successful and turbulent period in their history and I was to be part of it. As the club made history, I was there to photograph it, and this collection of images is a record of those amazing seasons: the two seasons when the club won promotion to the Scottish Premier Division, the Coca-Cola Cup triumph, and the side's UEFA Cup fortunes, which included the famous encounter with one of the biggest clubs in Europe.

I have always felt that it is an honour for any true supporter to be able to help his or her club. This book of photographs is dedicated to all true football supporters everywhere.

Tony Fimister
April 2002

Acknowledgements

All of the photographs used in this book were taken by the author, with the exception of the team group for the season 1995/96, which was taken by my son Barry Fimister and the photograph of me in action on the bottom of this page, which was taken by Marie Kyme.

Although this book started out as a solo effort, it wasn't until I started to write the acknowledgements that I realised how many people had helped me in some way or other. Some people helped me materially, others with information or simply with encouragement. To the following people I offer my thanks. The players of Raith Rovers Football Club since the start of the 1991/92 season. All the chairmen that I have worked for – Peter Campsie, Alex Penman, Alan Kelly, Douglas Cromb, William Gray and Danny Smith. The team managers – Jimmy Nicholl (twice), Jimmy Thomson, Tommy McLean (for about a week), Ian Munro, John McVeigh, Peter Hetherston and Jocky Scott. All their assistants and backroom staff. The office managers, Susan Rankin, Billy McPhee, Debbie Muir, Keri Gifford, Carrie Sommerville and all the clerical and commercial staff. The programme editors, Graeme Scott, Tom Murray, Paul Gilfillan, John Greechan, Colin Hume, John Litster and Allan Dall. Gordon Holmes, Bob Mackie and Bill Dickman of the *Fife Free Press*, (especially Bill, who once helped me out when I turned up at a game with the wrong speed of film). Ian Martin and his assistant video cameraman Ross Etherington – without Ian's help I would not have been able to produce a match video for every home game, which gave me more time to take photographs. I would also like to thank the club's ground staff and David Kirk for getting me started in photography in the first place.

Brian Jamieson of the Scottish Football League organised the permission that I required to reproduce items in this book and gave me a lot of encouragement. Klick Photopoint processing labs for their quick turnaround of all the reprints I required and for sorting out the problems. The ladies of the Klick Photopoint shop in Kirkcaldy for putting up with all the hassle. Vic Robertson of the Picture Gallery (Kirkcaldy) for all his time and technical advice, Kenny Stevenson of Edinburgh University, Jim Foy chairman of the supporters' club and most of all Catherine Fimister (my mum), who kept me going when I needed a push.

One

Early Days

The photograph that started it all for me as club photographer. Just a few days after I had taken a series of photographs of the stadium, I received a phone call from the office secretary, Susan Rankin, asking me if I would like to take over the position from Bob Mackie, who had joined the local newspaper.

The full squad line up for the 1991/92 team photo call. From left to right, back row: J. McStay, G. McGeachie, S. Crawford, R. Raeside, A. Buchanan, G. Arthur, A. Banner, I. Ferguson, G. Grant, T. Williamson, J. Dair. Middle row: J. Small (youth coach), D. Sinclair, S. Strang, S. Quinn, S. Kane, S. Dennis, G. Johnston, I. McLeod, M. Davis, P. Burn, D. Young, D. Dunleavy, M. Cheyne (trainer). Front row: D. Smith (coach), G. Dalziel, G. Gay, A. McKenzie, M. Cowan, R. Coyle, C. Cameron, J. Nicholl (manager), N. Henderson, C. Brewster, G. Meldrum, M. Nelson, S. Simpson, J. Valente (kit man).

Manager Jimmy Nicholl (centre) with his backroom staff. From left to right, Murray Cheyne, Joe Small, Jimmy, Derek Smith, John Valente.

An anxious moment for the defence in the Skol Cup second round tie against Motherwell. Raith went on to humble their Premier Division opponents, beating them 4-1 and setting themselves up for a money-spinning tie against Celtic at Parkhead in the next round.

Craig Brown, who was at that time assistant to Scotland manager Andy Roxburgh, chose Raith Rovers as the Skol Cup team of the second round. Manager Jimmy Nicholl accepts a cheque for £1,500 from a representative of the cup sponsors.

Situated behind the main stand and only open on match days, the Raith shop still managed to do brisk business. The shop is now the club's laundry room.

There was intense speculation surrounding Shaun Dennis and a possible £500,000 transfer to Celtic. It consequently came as something of a surprise to Raith Rovers fans when Ian Ferguson was snapped up by Hearts manager Joe Jordan in a deal worth over £100,000. Ian had been signed for Raith Rovers from Lochgelly Albert in 1987 by Jordan's assistant, Frank Connor. During his spell at Starks Park, Ian made 82 full appearances, with another 43 as substitute, and he managed a respectable tally of 23 goals.

In early November 1991, coach Murray Cheyne left the club and was replaced by former Northern Ireland international Martin Harvey, who took on the roll of assistant manager. Martin had been with Sunderland for twenty years, fifteen as a player and five as a reserve and youth team coach before moving to Carlisle as assistant to Bobby Moncur. When Moncur moved to Hearts, Martin took charge of the north-west side; however, he was sacked after only a year into the job. He again teamed up with Moncur, who was now in charge at Plymouth, where Martin spent the next ten years with the Pilgrims. Having won 34 caps for Northern Ireland, Martin had also served his country as assistant to Billy Bingham during the 1982 and 1986 World Cup finals – playing for Northern Ireland at that time was a certain Jimmy Nicholl …

Gordon Dalziel enhanced his goal-scoring reputation with a hat-trick against Morton in the third round of the B&Q Cup at Cappielow. Not only did Gordon please his manager and the fans, but he earned himself £100 worth of B&Q vouchers, three bottles of champagne and a kiss from B&Q's Jodie Taylor.

Every home match has a mascot, and against Forfar on the 1 February 1992 the lucky person was birthday boy Paul Freeman (can you guess his age?) Paul's favourite player was Peter 'Silky' Hetherston.

By the middle of March, Raith Rovers were sitting fourth in the table, only six points behind the leaders Dundee. The reserve team were sitting mid-table in the Reserve League East and the success of the senior side had rubbed off on the amateur team, who were able to fix up a sponsorship deal with the Abbotshall Hotel.

The junior supporters club sent two teams to Greenock for the Morton six-a-side tournament. The Under 16 team lost on penalties in their semi-final, but the Under 12s won the trophy in their section.

The mascot for the final game of the 1991/92 season was Wendy Graham. Wendy's address was given in the programme as being Cumbrae Terrace, Kirkcaldy, but for most people who knew Wendy, a true Raith fanatic, it should have been c/o Starks Park, as she was rarely seen away from the stadium.

Raith's first season as full-timers under manager Jimmy Nicholl ended with Rovers just above mid-table and only five points off the number one spot. The signs for the future were looking extremely hopeful. A 1-1 draw with Kilmarnock brought the curtain down, Allan McKenzie sending a rocket into the 'Killie' net for Raith's goal.

No season can be complete without the obligatory end of season awards. Top of the list had to be Gordon Dalziel *(left)*, with his tally including the PFA Players' Player of the Year award, the Raith Players' Player of the Year award, the B&Q Super Skills award for the First Division and the supporters' club Player of the Year award. A star of the future, Jason Dair *(right)*, won the supporters' club Young Player of the Year award.

Two

A Dream Start

The first team pool for 1992/93. From left to right, back row: D. Young, D. Sinclair, P. Hetherston, G. Arthur, C. Brewster, T. Williamson. S. Strang. Middle row: D. Dunleavy, J. McStay, I. McLeod, S. Dennis, R. Raeside, R. Coyle, G. McGeachie, P. Burn. Front row: J. Valente (kit man), A. McKenzie, G. Docherty (physio.), J. Nicholl, M. Harvey (assistant manager), G. Dalziel, J. Small (youth coach).

Jimmy Nicholl has a go at my job. Luckily for me, Jimmy stuck to managing the team and left me to take the photographs.

The start of a new season and the slog to peak fitness. It was up the road for the squad to Beveridge Park for a few circuits around the park's perimeter track. You'll note that although the players were quite capable of beating the 'gaffer' to the finishing line, not one was brave enough to risk it!

The pre-season friendlies kicked off on 18 July with a visit from Hearts, who were followed three days later by their Edinburgh neighbours, Hibs. Here, Hearts' Scott Crabbe seems to have the ball glued to the sole of his boot while being closely marked by Davy Sinclair.

More friendlies followed and Raith took on a Rangers select at Starks Park before travelling through to Methil for the Fife cup tournament, beating East Fife 3-1 in the semi-final and recording a 1-0 victory over Dunfermline in the final. Colin 'Mickey' Cameron proudly shows off the Fife Cup before the friendly against Aberdeen. Little did Colin or the assembled Raith fans know that this was just a dress rehearsal for far more important trophies to be held by one of the best players to come out of Starks Park in years.

TODAY'S MATCH SPONSOR

FORDS
SOLICITORS

FOLLOWING RAITH ROVERS TO THE PREMIER LEAGUE

FOR PREMIER ADVICE CONTACT US

WE OFFER A FULL RANGE OF LEGAL SERVICES WITH FRIENDLY AND PROMPT SERVICE

21 tolbooth street,
Kirkcaldy KY1 1RW
Tel: (0592) 640630
Fax: (0592) 640622

A dream start was how Jimmy Nicholl described the 7-0 thrashing of St Mirren. Goals from Gordon Dalziel (3), Craig Brewster (2), Jason Dair and Ronnie Coyle had the fans floating high above the stadium on cloud nine. It was a certainly a dream start, but what use are dreams if they don't come true now and then? This dream was to turn into reality. The match sponsors' advert on page nineteen of the programme seemed to be able to predict something special. As well as offering a full range of legal services, perhaps Nigel Ford should have included crystal ball reading in his advert.

Gordon Dalziel slips the ball past the St Mirren goalkeeper Campbell Money for the first of his three goals.

Craig Brewster out-jumps the Saints' defence.

A slightly shell-shocked Gordon Dalziel receives the man of the match award from sponsor Nigel Ford. Because of the team's outstanding performance, the sponsor offered to give a bottle of whisky to all the players who took part in the match. This offer was rejected by Pete Rodger, the club's commercial manager. You have to wonder what the rest of the team made of that decision …

After the euphoria of the St Mirren game, Raith settled into a familiar pattern. A 0-0 draw at home to Stirling Albion brought the fans and the team back down to earth. This was followed by a respectable 1-1 draw away to Kilmarnock and although Premier Division Hibernian defeated Raith 1-4 in the Skol Cup at Easter Road, the defeat, while heavy, gave everyone hope for the league campaign as the team had acquitted themselves well. Narrow wins against Ayr 1-0, Dunfermline 1-0 and Dumbarton 2-1 saw Raith sitting proudly at the top of the First Division. Hamilton Accies were the next team to try and dent the promotion push. Accies took a sixth-minute lead through Paul McDonald, but with eleven minutes on the clock, Craig Brewster hit the equaliser.

It was left to Ian Thomson to hit the winner when he crashed a superb Gordon Dalziel cross off the underside of the bar. Ian Thomson had been a £20,000 steal from Queen of the South. This fee was set at an SFL tribunal, as both clubs had disagreed over the player's value.

With only one Premier League game on in Scotland, due to an international game in Switzerland, the media were out in force for the game against Hamilton. BBC Radio Scotland had sent along their top team of commentators, Bob Crampsey (a former Brain of Britain) and Alistair Alexander to broadcast the game to the nation.

Not to be outdone, a team of presenters from the local hospital radio service, VRN, relayed a commentary by landline to patients in the town's Victoria Hospital. The Victoria Radio Network line-up was, from left to right, Alan Davidson, David Potter, Murray Morgan.

Groundsman and former player Andy Leigh played his part in the team's success by keeping the stadium in pristine condition.

The Starks Park pitch was like a championship snooker table, and it more than matched the quality of play that the team were producing.

When Morton paid a visit to Kirkcaldy, they were sitting in second place, only two points behind Raith. David Wylie in the Morton goal played out of his skin during the match.

A ballboy jumps into shot, but who could blame him as he celebrates Gordon Dalziel's equaliser after Rowan Alexander had given Morton an early lead. Craig Brewster scored the winner as Raith went on to win 2-1.

Raith's fine unbeaten run at home finally came to an end, but thankfully not in the league. Meadowbank Thistle were our opponents in the second round of the B&Q Cup. Due to a lengthy injury list and a 'flu virus that had swept through the club, Raith had to field a weakened team. After ninety minutes of normal play, the score still stood at 0-0 and with no one able to break the deadlock in extra time, the game was settled with a penalty shoot-out. Unfortunately, Meadowbank won this 2-4 – what a way to settle a cup tie!

Seven-year-old mascot Christopher Forrest shows off his coin tossing technique before the kick-off against Dumbarton. Christopher turned out to be a very lucky mascot for Raith as they ran out 4-1 winners.

The fact that Raith were the last unbeaten team in British league football that year had been brought to the attention of the national press and the *Daily Mail* sent a reporter and cameraman from London to cover the match against Dumbarton. The reporter was an exiled 'Rovers' fan called Alan Fraser and the cameraman, Ted Blackbrow, caused a bit of a sensation by climbing up the south-west pylon during the game to get a panoramic shot of the stadium and the bay area of Kirkcaldy. Surely no photographer could ever be daft enough to climb up one of those pylons just to get a photograph …?

Zena Johnstone from Markinch featured as the fan of the month. Zena had been a Raith Rovers fan since the 1940s and she became an active member of the supporters' club and served on the committee for a number of years. Asked by the programme editor Tom Murray who was her favourite player over the years, Zena replied that she regarded football as a team game where individuals always come second.

Derby games are always special occasions, especially when they are against the 'Pars'. Visitors Dunfermline were third in the league, six points behind Raith, but after the 1-0 home victory, the team from the west of Fife had slipped back to fourth place. Here, Jock McStay is making his presence felt.

A section of the reported 5,200 crowd who saw Raith triumph by a solitary goal from Stephen Crawford.

The following Saturday Raith's other west Fife rivals, Cowdenbeath, paid us a visit and brought heavy rain with them. The boys in the dug out seemed happy enough with their cover and the 3-0 win.

Spare a thought for the poor BBC cameraman and sound man who had no protection from the elements as they worked on the temporary television gantry on the railway stand enclosure.

Fans' favourite Gordon Dalziel was granted a testimonial season by the club. A committee headed by John Brown held a dinner in the town's Dean Park hotel as part of the celebrations. The dinner attracted an audience of over three hundred people. Included in the guest list were Rangers stars Richard Gough (left) and Ally McCoist (right).

In the run up to Christmas and New Year, things were hectic both on and off the park, especially for office secretary Susan Rankin (seated) and her match-day assistant Moira Campsie.

Our ever-efficient ballboys, Huw Thomas, Steven Douglas, Philip Arnold, Steven Woods, John Clark and Ross Fyfe, were well kitted out for the winter weather.

A new deal with McDonald's burger chain to sponsor the match-day mascots was launched just before the New Year. Some of the players paid a visit to the High Street branch of McDonald's to meet the fans and sample the merchandise.

By the time Stirling Albion paid their second visit of the season to Starks Park, Raith were sitting on top of the league table, seven points clear of their nearest rivals, Dunfermline. Gordon Arthur was back in goal and a fully fit Shaun Dennis was on top of his form.

Stephen Crawford opened the scoring for Raith.

The home fans were treated to a superb run down the left wing by full back Ian Mcleod.

'Marshall' Mcleod jinked past a defender, shot at goal, and made the points safe for the 'Rovers'.

Long-term injury victim Shaun Dennis was back to full fitness and manager Jimmy Nicholl was hoping that Shaun's return to the first team would give the team that extra dimension in the run up to the last quarter of the season.

Players Ronnie Coyle (pictured) and Craig Brewster both signed full-time contracts for the club. It was hoped that their added involvement would also help the team's promotion push.

The answer to the question about who would be daft enough to climb up one of the pylons just to get a photograph is ... the author! Maybe it was because the team were reaching such great heights or maybe I had just lost control of my senses, but I decided to climb the north-west pylon to try and produce a photograph of the stadium. It was a calm day, there was not even a slight breeze as I climbed the hooped ladder bolted onto the side of that imposing structure. When I managed to reach the gantry, I found to my horror that the pylon sways back and forth even on the calmest of days – so much so, in fact, that I had to hold on to a support with one hand and fire off a few frames while holding the camera in the other hand. One-handed photography is never advisable, but is the only option when you're taking pictures from a moving gantry, high above the ground.

The result of the author's heroics was worth it (but never again!).

The Morton game and the infamous overhead kick. Gordon Dalziel was fast approaching his thirty-first birthday and also the chance to win the *Daily Record*'s Silver Shot award for being the first player to score thirty goals. (Rangers Ally McCoist had scooped the Golden award back in November). The prize to the lucky, or should I say skilful player, was £500 and a case of champagne. Raith were in full control of the game throughout, with Morton pegged back into their own half for most of the match. Peter Hetherston sent over this corner kick in the 23rd minute.

Gordon's overhead kick into the Morton net was a classic goal, one that would be remembered by the Starks Park faithful for many years to come. Seven days later, Gordon scored goal number thirty to win the Silver Shot Award and no doubt share the prizes with his team-mates.

Three

The Path to Glory

A few weeks after joining the club, I was invited to Jimmy Nicholl's home to take a photograph of Jimmy, his wife Susan and their three daughters. Over a cup of coffee, Jimmy explained some of the problems that football managers have running a club like Raith Rovers with limited resources. During the conversation, I asked whether it would be helpful if one of my colleagues videoed the home matches for him and his players to study. Since then, every senior match at Starks Park has been recorded, mainly by Ian Martin, who is pictured here seen here working from the Railway Stand.

A slightly more advanced camera crew took over the filming for the visit of Kilmarnock in mid-March. A full BBC outside broadcast unit (Jock Brown and all) was in place to see if Tommy Burns' team would be able to halt Raith's drive to the Premier Division.

The BBC's Dougie Donnelly referred to Peter Hetherston as having 'a good engine'. The programme editor was slightly more accurate when he described Peter as producing Rolls-Royce displays, as he did here against Killie's Billy Stark.

To be fair, Rolls-Royce displays apart, it was 'goals for' that the Rovers fans were after and Craig Brewster duly obliged after a shot from Jimmy Nicholl had spun in the air. Craig was first to react to drive the ball past Bobby Geddes.

Much to the delight of Jock McStay and Gordon Dalziel, Gordon went on to settle the match with a second goal, his thirtieth of the season – this was the goal that won him the Silver Shot award.

Just a week after that crucial win against Kilmarnock and Raith were at home to second-placed Dunfermline. A win for the home side would surely seal the title for the Kirkcaldy side, but a win for the 'Pars' wouldn't just mean two league points, but also a massive confidence boost for the visitors. A typical derby game filled with more tension than skill saw Craig Brewster threaten a resolute Dunfermline defence, but it was two goals from Jimmy Nicholl, one straight from a corner kick, that kept the points in Kirkcaldy.

After two matches on the road, against Ayr 0-0 and Hamilton 2-2, Dumbarton made the trip to Kirkcaldy and as the team bus drew up at Starks Park, the crowds were already stretched down Pratt Street to the Links. This was a rare sight as it's usually only cup ties against Rangers or Celtic that inspire the Kirkcaldy fans to come out in large numbers, but the fans had one thing on their minds that afternoon. Raith needed a win, and if the other results went their way, then the club could be celebrating promotion to the Premier Division for the first time in our history. The long queues delayed the kick-off by ten minutes.

The mascots for the Dumbarton game were twelve-year-old David Tracey from Linlithgow (second from the left) and Jock McStay's son Jonathon, who is beingheld by Gordon Dalziel.

It wasn't until the 27th minute that Craig Brewster opened the scoring. The Sons' 'keeper Ian McFarlane was in sparkling form and had pulled off three excellent saves in a row before Craig thundered in a low shot from outside the penalty box that gave the goalie no chance.

Gordon Dalziel looked certain to score when Raith won a penalty after he had been brought down by Dumbarton's Paul Martin, a foul that referee Bill Crombie thought merited a red card. Gordon scored from the spot kick, but the referee ordered a re-take and took Ian McLeod's name for encroachment. In-form Ian McFarlane brilliantly saved the second attempt to leave Raith going in with just a one goal advantage at half time.

It took Craig Brewster only three minutes in the second half to put Raith two up; from then on, Rovers just cruised through the game against the ten men of Dumbarton. With radios pressed to ears all around the stadium, a huge cheer went up when ten minutes from the end of this game, but almost on the final whistle at all the other grounds, the news came through that Clydebank's Craig Flanagan had scored a late equaliser against Dunfermline. Even the team on the bench joined in the chants of 'Championies-Championies'.

The fans were chanting 'You won't keep us off the pitch' and as the referee blew the final whistle a good hearted crowd stormed over the barriers and invaded the pitch. At one point Jimmy Nicholl (wearing a policeman's helmet) was being carried shoulder high through the crowd.

The dressing room was rockin'.

The champagne flowed ...

Raith skipper Peter 'Silky' Hetherston climbed onto the wall in front of the directors' box to salute the fans who had played their part in securing the team's unexpected rise to the top.

Jimmy Nicholl, surrounded by his players, savours the moment and reflects on the past games that had taken his team to the Premier Division.

Gordon Dalziel shares some of the champagne with the crowd – but where did he get that hat?

The First Division Championship was in the bag, but there were still fixtures to complete. After a 1-1 draw at Cappielow, it was back to Starks Park and a local derby with the 'Blue Brazil'. Cowdenbeath players applauded the Raith team onto the pitch before the presentation of the First Division trophy.

Skipper Peter Hetherston receives the trophy from League management treasurer Eric Campbell, watched by League secretary Peter Donald and club chairman Peter Campsie.

The skipper and the gaffer proudly hold the trophy that they and their team had worked so hard and waited so long for. This was a great honour for the club and for the people of Kirkcaldy.

There was still a game to play and Raith easily beat an already relegated Cowdenbeath 4-1. Gordon Dalziel scored two of the goals.

The Championship-winning team. From left to right, back row: John McStay, Stephen Crawford, Robert Raeside, Shaun Dennis, George McGeachie, Ian Thomson. Middle row: Martin Harvey (assistant manager), Jason Dair, Gordon Arthur, Ian McLeod, Tom Carson, David Sinclair, Gerry Docherty (physio.). Front row: Craig Brewster, Ian MacKenzie, Peter Hetherston, Jimmy Nicholl, Gordon Dalziel, Ronnie Coyle, Colin Cameron.

Gordon Dalziel is applauded onto the pitch by his fellow team-mates and the players of St Johnstone, who provide the opposition for his testimonial game. On the right of the photo is Gordon's daughter Nicola and on the left, his niece, Melanie Hemphill. Gordon Dalziel had been a great asset to Raith Rovers from the time that Frank Connor had persuaded him to join the club instead of giving up the game. To add to the the league championship medal, Gordon had again been awarded the PFA Players' Player of the Year award.

Before the annual awards ceremony, the players had a chance to relax, let their hair down and, by the look of things, keep Budweiser in business.

Brian Fairfull, chairman of the supporters' club, presents Raith Rover's chairman Peter Campsie with a crystal decanter to commemorate the football club's achievements.

Peter Hetherston, Craig Brewster and Colin Cameron scooped the supporters' club player awards. Craig also picked up the ABC 'starcheck' award from the *Fife Free Press*. The photograph shows, from left to right, Allan Melville (Supporters Club), Peter Hetherston, Craig Brewster, Colin Cameron and Fraser Hamilton (Supporters Club).

Scottish League Division 1

Raith Rovers	44	25	4	15	85	41	65
Kilmarnock	44	21	11	12	67	40	54
Dunfermline	44	22	14	8	64	47	52
St Mirren	44	21	14	9	62	52	51
Hamilton	44	19	13	12	65	45	50
Morton	44	19	15	10	65	56	48
AyrUnited	44	14	12	18	49	44	46
Clydebank	44	16	15	13	71	66	45
Dumbarton	44	15	22	7	56	71	37
Stirling Albion	44	11	20	13	44	61	35
Meadowbank	44	11	23	10	51	80	32
Cowdenbeath	44	3	34	7	33	109	13

The final league placings for the First Division for the 1992/93 season.

Four

The 'Windae Hingers'

The first team pool for the 1993/94 season. From left to right, back row: M. Quinn, S. Crawford, J. Dair, D. Sinclair, J. Rowbotham, M. Buist, C. Cameron, J. Broddle, S. McBain. Middle row: I. McMillan, W. Hawke, G. McNab, T. Carson, G. McGeachie, G. Arthur, I. McLeod, R. Coyle, I. Thomson, J. Valente (kit man). Front row: G. Docherty (physio.), S. Dennis, J. McStay, J. Nicholl (manager), P. Hetherston, G. Dalziel, M. Harvey (assistant manager).

At the previous season's photocall only three photographers turned up, but Raith's success attracted the national media and fifteen 'snappers' made their way to Starks Park.

Partial ground reconstruction was under way during the summer of 1993. The 'home' end was the first part of the stadium to be given a facelift. Unfortunately, the levelling of the south terracing by Kirkcaldy contractor John Leitch emphasised the pitch's slope even more.

It was car sponsorship time and Jimmy Nicholl is seen here collecting his Mazda 626 from dealership manager Kenny Stevenson (left) and owner Murray Grubb (right).

Club captain Peter Hetherston picked up the keys to his Vauxhall Cavalier from S.V.L. sales manager Robbie Stewart. On the left of the picture is the club's commercial manager Pete Rodger, who had negotiated the deal.

Diadora were the new kit suppliers and Christine Smith (left) and Julie Rutherford (right) modelled the new tops. Ruth Addison (centre) showed off the very popular 'Pure Genius' T-shirt.

Colin Cameron, Robert Raeside and David Sinclair line up for a photograph with some young Raith fans who turned up for the club's open day. Unfortunately, just after this photograph was taken, Robbie Raeside badly injured his knee when his studs caught in the lush turf during one of the playing sessions with the fans. The injury required surgery.

Kelly's Copiers of Dundee were signed up as main sponsor for Raith's first season in the Premier Division. The group are, from left to right, back row: Kelly's sales director Ken Forrest, Shaun Dennis, John McStay, Raith Rovers honorary treasurer and director Terry Watt. Front row: Stuart Young (commercial director for Kelly's), Alan Paul of Northern Promotions (who helped broker the deal), Raith chairman Peter Campsie.

Youth coach Derek Smith was understandably very proud of the youth squad who had returned from the Manchester United International Football Festival, having won the Under 16 section, scoring a total of 40 goals and conceding only 2. In the final, the team triumphed by 2 goals to 1 over I.K. Frej of Sweden.

Raith's pre-season preparations got under way with a whistle-stop tour of Ireland, then back home to play Luton. The early work out was concluded with the Fife Cup tournament, which was being played at Starks Park this season. Cowdenbeath had managed a 5-4 penalty shoot-out win over Dunfermline in the first of the semi-finals. Raith took on a very enthusiastic Burntisland Shipyard in the other semi-final, predictably beating them 3-1.

In the final, Raith had to come back from being two goals to one down against the Central Park side to win 5-2.

Before Raith's first ever Premier Division match, Kirkcaldy's Provost, Robert King, presented chairman Peter Campsie with a Kirkcaldy town crest in recognition for winning promotion to the top league.

The team line up before the start of the match with St Johnstone to watch Peter Campsie, accompanied by the secretary of the Scottish League, Peter Donald, unfurl the 1992/93 First Division league championship flag.

John McStay tries for a piggyback on St Johnstone's goal scorer Paul Wright. Shaun Dennis was the Raith scorer in the 1-1 draw that started the club's league campaign.

That 1-1 draw was all the fans had to cheer as we prepared to welcome Partick Thistle to Kirkcaldy, having lost 0-1 to Hearts at Tynecastle and then being knocked out of the League Cup 1-2 at home to Arbroath. An exciting end to end game finished 2-2, with Gordon Dalziel scoring his first Premiership goal.

They say that when policemen start to look young, you're getting old. How do you think I felt when I saw this 'young' photographer on duty at a Raith v. Celtic reserve game?

I put my feelings of old age behind me and captured a very happy looking Stevie McBain in action against the 'Hoops' reserves.

George McGeachie keeps his eye on Charlie Nicholas. Charlie won the man of the match award for Celtic as he turned in a vintage performance, scoring twice in the 4-1 defeat of Raith. This was a defeat that ended the home side's proud 18-month unbeaten home league record.

Stephen Crawford worked well with Colin Cameron to score Rovers' only goal of the game.

Ticket or no ticket, these 'windae hingers' weren't going to miss any of the Raith v. Celtic action.

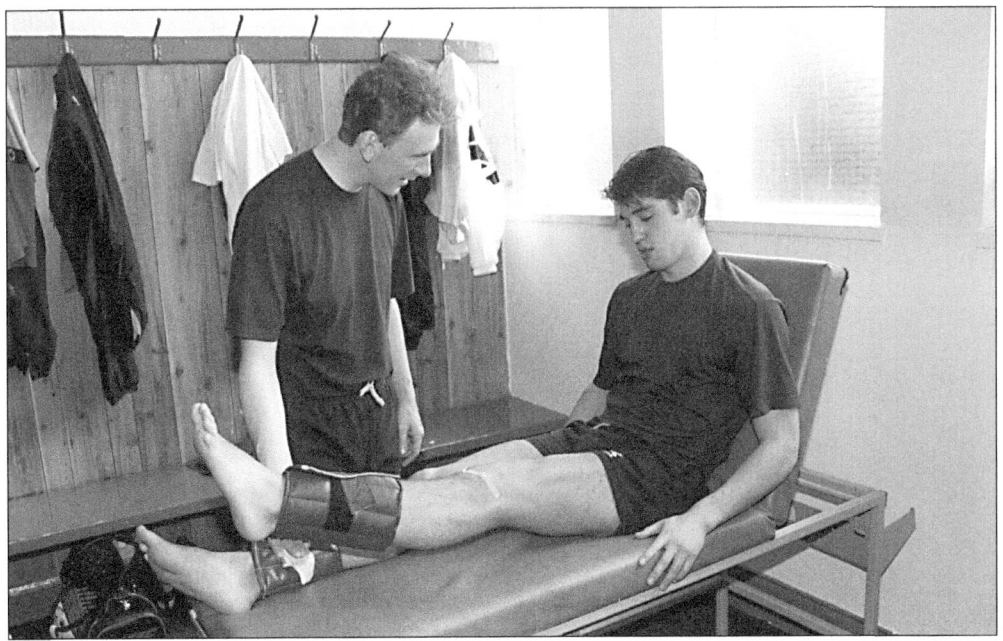

Bad news for Robbie Raeside. A return to hospital showed that ligament damage to his injured knee would require a further operation, consequently delaying his return to action. Club physiotherapist Gerry Docherty had spent much of his time bringing Robbie back from a career-threatening injury.

By the time Rangers paid a visit to Starks Park, Raith were second bottom of the Premier Division with only one win and three draws out of eight starts. The team were obviously missing the strength, height and skill of Craig Brewster, who had decided to move to Dundee United at the start of the season. Mindful of the need to freshen up the team, manager Jimmy Nicholl signed two new players. Goalkeeper Scott Thomson signed from Forfar, with Gordon Arthur moving to Station Park as part of the deal. Ally Graham was the other new face in the line-up. Unfortunately, Ally's debut lasted only into the early part of the first half. Having made a great start to the game, a looping header from Ally rebounded off the Rangers crossbar and as Raith pushed forward, Ally went down under a pile of defenders.

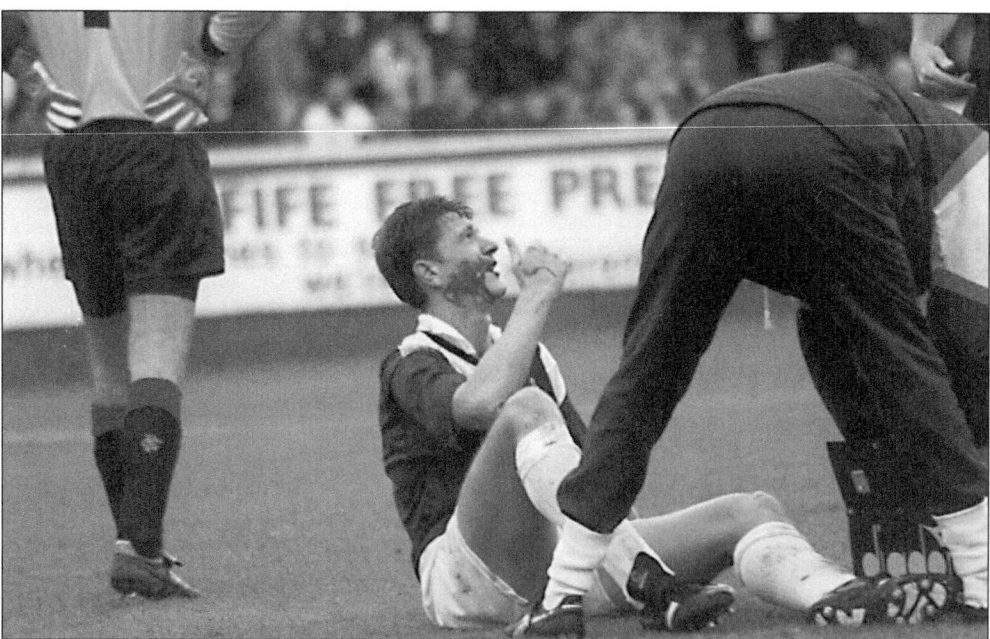

After the bodies were cleared, Ally was left with a badly cut lip and three broken teeth.

A patched-up Ally Graham scored his first goal for his new team in the next home fixture against Kilmarnock, heading home a superb Dalziel cross.

Peter Hetherston crashes a low shot into the Hearts net in this 1-0 victory over their Edinburgh visitors. This was Raith's first league win of the season.

Club mascot Lee Sharp brought some luck to the team in their match against Dundee as Raith won 2-1. Lee was photographed with his favourite players, Jock McStay and Ally Graham.

The mascot for the game against Hibs was Ian Bell of Kinglassie, who had a new hero in goalie Scott Thomson.

Although the campaign on the field wasn't going too well for the team, due to too many drawn games, the hospitality suites were kept busy.

Some of the staff who kept the customers happy before and after the match. From left to right, Karen, June, Gillian, Sheila and Carol.

The players forgot about their lowly league position to let their hair down at the players' Christmas party.

Julian Broddle, Ally Graham, Ian McMillan and Stevie Crawford belt it out at the karaoke machine.

Jock McStay and Shaun Dennis enjoy a drink.

Gordon Dalziel contemplates what to do with a stuffed ostrich.

By late November, the cold weather had started to effect the fixtures and caused a double postponement. Even the pitch covers couldn't help.

Groundsman Andy Leigh and his assistant Tony Coventry were helpless against the wintry conditions.

Five

Too Many Draws

On his first ever visit to Starks Park, long-distance Rovers fan of thirty-four years Peter Ackland made the trip up to Kirkcaldy from Barnstaple in Devon to see the team that he had adopted all those years ago. Peter was so taken with the Kirkcaldy club that he had even named his son Raith. Pictured here with Raith, Peter described his journey to the Lang Toun as a dream come true.

By the time Dundee United crossed the Tay to pay us a visit on league business, Raith were eleventh (second from bottom) in the table, but only three points off the safety of fourth place. Unfortunately, too many draws had been the Raith's downfall and United were in no mood to stop that. When the Raith forwards did manage a shot on goal, they found Guido Van De Kamp in sparkling form.

Even the hard running of Colin Cameron couldn't help to avoid a 2-0 defeat.

The Scottish Cup gave the fans a wee break from the disappointment of the league campaign and Brechin City in their all red strip certainly brightened a dull February day. Raith went into a two-goal lead in the first half through Jason Dair (24 minutes) and Jock McStay (31 minutes), and despite some near misses, the game finished 2-0 to Raith and a trip to Aberdeen in the fourth round was to be the team's reward.

Fan of the month for February was a very fit looking Jessie Hamilton. Jessie had lived in David Street for many years and was now a resident in the Raith Gates home. Born only eleven years after Raith Rovers were formed, Jessie described herself as a life-long supporter – in fact she had last been at a match at Starks Park in September of 1992 when she was ninety-eight years old. Stephen Crawford, Jason Dair and Davy Sinclair paid Jessie a visit on her 100th birthday on Sunday 30 January. Rumours that Davy borrowed Jessie's Zimmer frame for the gaffer were never confirmed – or denied!

That victory against Brechin had given the team a boost and a week later they put on a tremendous display against Celtic. The programme editor said in the following edition that if the game had been a boxing match, Raith would have easily won on points. The boys in blue, as opposed to the 'bhoys' in green, had Celtic on the ropes for most of the game, but as luck would have it they couldn't produce the knockout punch. Even a very tricky John Collins wasn't able to get the better of Raith's Stephen Crawford and the game ended 0-0.

Following two trips to Aberdeen, the first in the league (0-4) and the second, seven days later, in the fourth round of the Scottish Cup (0-1), Raith had to face league leaders Rangers. The Rovers were on top in the early stages of this game and only bad luck stopped them from taking an early lead through Colin Cameron. In fifteen minutes, Davy Sinclair sent Stephen Crawford through on goal and the youngster made no mistake, much to the delight of Ally Graham, Colin Cameron and the home support. The match then adopted a familiar pattern, and goals from Ian Ferguson (on 72 minutes) and Gordon Durie (on 79 minutes) killed off the game and the points went west.

Player-manager Jimmy Nicholl (no Zimmer frame in sight) celebrates Colin Cameron's goal, which put Raith two goals to one ahead in this league encounter with Hearts. Referee Martindale then yellow-carded 'Mickey' for celebrating his goal with the Hearts fans. Although the Rovers were well on top for most of the game, they couldn't kill off the 'Jambos' and a late goal by Craig Levein earned Hearts a share of the points.

A competition run in the match-day programme was won by a young lady from Edinburgh, Eilidh Ross. The prize was a framed, autographed programme, complete with the original photograph which made up the front cover. The photograph was an action shot of Rangers' Gary Stevens and Raith's Jason Dair and both players had autographed the front cover of the programme before the last Raith v. Rangers fixture. The prize was presented to Eilidh by Jason Dair and Nigel Ford of Fords Solicitors, who had sponsored the competition.

New signing Danny Lennon makes an encouraging debut for Raith against fellow strugglers Dundee. In an even game, Shaw scored first for the visitors before Stephen Crawford grabbed an equaliser in the 51st minute.

Scott Thomson, Mickey Cameron and their quiz team partners rack their brains for answers at the 'meet the players' night held in the Raith Suite. The question that had them stumped was most probably 'Whose round is it?'

Former Raith favourite Keith Wright opened the scoring for Hibs on a cold and windy Tuesday night on 26 April. Keith and Shaun Dennis had a great tussle throughout the game, but it was only fair when Ronnie Coyle flighted the ball right to Ally Graham, who headed a square ball into the Hibs box. Peter Hetherston dummied and Colin Cameron swept a low shot past Jim Leighton to make the final score 1-1.

Match sponsor for the last home game of the season and the last in the Premier Division (at least for a wee while) was Hussman Refrigeration. John Mitchell and his guests enjoyed the hospitality of the club and an exciting six-goal thriller served up by both teams.

The new board of directors look on as Raith played out the season with relegation a certainty. Alex Penman had taken control of the club and he was already preparing for the new season back in the First Division.

The 'Steel Men' were second from the top of the division and Raith were second from the bottom, having failed to take a single point from Tommy McLean's men all season. With nothing left to play for except pride, Raith threw everything they had at Motherwell and Motherwell threw it all back. Jason Dair worked his socks off, as did all the players, and Raith managed to finally take a point off the visitors in an exciting 3-3 draw. Raith's final game that season was away to Dundee United, Peter Hetherston's last for the club. With a young Brian Potter in goal, Raith managed a magnificent 3-2 win to say farewell to the big league. After the excitement of winning promotion the previous season, the Rovers faithful were down but far from out. They were proud, very proud of what this small Scottish provincial team had achieved in such a short time. If it hadn't been for all those drawn games, especially at home, things, might have been so different ... Raith's record reads:

P	W	D	L	F	A	Pts
44	6	19	19	46	80	31

Not to worry, there's always next season ...

Six

Blue Cans of Coke
1994/95

Raith's first attempt at playing with the big boys may not have been a roaring success on the pitch, but it did result in some improvements to the ground, such as a brand new public address system, which was funded by the supporters' club. On the microphone was a certain Drew Nairn, often regarded as one of the best stadium announcers in Scottish football.

The full playing staff for 1994/95 with the first team squad in the very popular red and blue striped kit. David Kirkwood, third from the right on the front, is seen sporting a blue and white strip. This didn't mean that David was a reserve (or youth) player – there just wasn't enough of the striped kit to go around.

The club's main sponsor for the season was Jackie O's nightclub, a well-known nightspot in the town. Beverley McKenzie, the manageress of the club, brought some of her staff to the photocall to model the new strip.

Pre-season training – or is Danny Lennon practising the conga?

Jimmy Nicoll welcomes Bryan Robson and his Middlesbrough team to Starks Park for a pre-season friendly.

Our first match in the Premier Division in 1993/94 had been a 1-1 home draw against St Johnstone and history repeated itself with an identical fixture and scoreline to start the new season. Colin Cameron, who was fast becoming the hottest property in Scottish football, scored Raith's goal and was named man of the match.

'Keeper Scott Thomson was also on top of his form, pulling off some amazing saves.

Adding to the crowd of 2,825 was a group of West Bromwich Albion supporters. The fans of the 'Baggies' travelled up to Kirkcaldy on a free Saturday in their fixture list to take in a Rovers' match and to visit former West Brom player Willie Johnston, who is a publican in Kirkcaldy.

After forty-six years' service to the club, former player and groundsman Andy Leigh decided to call it a day and he took down the nets for the final time after the St Johnstone game.

Raith's two new signings, David Narey (left) and Ian Redford (right) pose for this photograph with the match mascot prior to the Coca-Cola third round tie with Kilmarnock. The side had already travelled to Dingwall for the second round tie, where they had seen off Ross County 5-0 (a great score, which included an Ally Graham hat-trick). The home fans were treated to an amazing cup game and another three goal hero in the shape of Colin Cameron as Raith progressed to the next round, winning 3-2.

With a new board of directors in place at Starks Park, led by local builder Alex Penman, changes were taking place in all departments of the club. Alex Kilgour had replaced Pete Rodger as commercial manager, Billy McPhee was appointed general manager and in an effort to bring in more revenue, a club shop was opened at the west end of the High Street.

By the time Clydebank paid us a visit on the first Saturday in September, Raith were sitting third bottom of the league with only two points from three games, the best results apparently reserved for the cup run. On a dull afternoon, Colin 'Mickey' Cameron was again Raith's best player and he scored the side's only goal in a 1-1 draw.

Big striker Ally Graham was hot on the heels of Mickey in the goal-scoring contest, although he too was saving his best for the cup.

Raith Rovers have fans all over the world, mostly exiled Langtonians, but we were about to add a couple of Australians to our growing list of admirers. Scott Michaelson, who played Brad in the Australian soap opera *Neighbours*, paid a visit to our main sponsors, Jackie O's, to meet some of the fans. Scott was presented with a Raith strip by Beverley McKenzie, manageress of the nightclub, who chose to give him a white third strip (to show off his tan).

Jackie O's other foreign visitor was Scott's fellow *Neighbours* star, Natalie Imbruglia. Natalie was touring the UK clubs prior to launching her singing career. There was no Raith strip for Natalie, but she did have the opportunity to meet some of players. From left to right: Trevor Williamson (no longer a Raith player, but on a visit to see the team), Colin Cameron, Beverley McKenzie, Natalie Imbruglia, Robbie Raeside.

Rovers finally broke their run of drawn league matches away to St Mirren. Then, on 1 October, with Ayr United the visitors, they notched up their first home league win of the season, beating Ayr 3-1. Substitute Gordon Dalziel scored twice, one goal being a well-taken penalty.

It was back to drawn games when Dundee came to Starks Park. The defence were on top form in this 1-1 draw. Scott Thomson in the Raith goal had to brave some awkward challenges, sometimes from his own forwards.

I don't often take photographs at away matches as the club doesn't really have a use for them. However, after Raith had knocked St Johnstone out of the Coca-Cola Cup on their own patch 3-1 and were drawn to play Airdrie in the cup semi-finals up at McDiarmid Park, I decided to take my cameras up to Perth and get in some location practice before the big event. St Johnstone were still smarting from their previous encounter with Raith and they produced a fine performance, reversing the score from the cup game. Davy Sinclair did manage to reach new heights for Raith that day, however.

I'm not usually superstitious, but when I was handed the number thirteen bib at McDiarmuid Park on Cup semi-final day, I had visions of impending disaster for Raith. That night, Raith drew 1-1 with Cup specialists Airdire, having lost 'keeper Scott Thomson in a dubious red card decision in the second half. The side survived extra time and won through 5-4 on penalties, with our young reserve 'keeper, Brian Potter, the hero of the night. The next day, I found that the bib had been unlucky: a technical fault in the processing ruined all but one of my photographs of that historic night. But at least the surviving picture was of Raith's new hero, and the club were going to be in a cup final!

Back to league duty and the struggle for points ... After the epic win against Airdrie in the cup, a derby game awaited the team and their fans when Dunfermline made the short trip to Starks Park. It looked as if Raith were about to overrun the Pars when the home side went two goals up, but Dunfermline had other ideas. Maybe it was the stamina-sapping extra time and penalties of the previous game that had taken its toll, but Raith collapsed and Dunfermline ran out worthy winners by 5-2. Cup-tied Barry Wilson scored both Raith goals and was almost strangled into the bargain.

October had been a great month for the club and Jimmy Nicholl was duly rewarded for his efforts by being named Bells manager of the month. United Distiller's Turnbull Hutton, a confessed Rovers fan, presented Jimmy with his award.

After the 2-5 home defeat at the hands of Dunfermline, the cup finalists pulled up their socks and produced three wins a row to put themselves into fourth place in the league, eleven points behind Airdrie but with a game in hand (three points were now awarded for a win). Understandably, the week running up to the cup final was a blur of activity at the club. Media interviews and photocalls kept the players busy in between training and tactics talks. Even giant blue and white Coke cans came onto the scene.

It wasn't just the current team who enjoyed the run-up to cup final day. United Distillers had produced a special blend of whisky to toast Raith's biggest day since the League Cup final against Rangers in 1949. Veterans of the 1949 final were invited to sample the blend and to a man voted the product, named 'The Final Blend', a winner. The line-up in the photograph is, from left to right: Harry Colville, Willie Penman, Turnbull Hutton of United Distillers, Andy Leigh. Seated: Johnny Maule.

Seven

Would a Captain Miss?

The big day had arrived. Thousands of Raith Rovers fans (I wonder where they all came from?) made their way to Ibrox, hoping, praying, some even expecting a miracle. One fan, Allan Elder, had even flown in from Chicago for the final. They didn't know it at the time, but a miracle was about to happen, a dream was about to come true. Millions watched on television or tuned in to their radios for coverage of the match, but it was the 11,000 blue-and-white-clad fans in the Govan stand that really counted. A team's twelfth man had never worked so hard to help the team triumph.

Raith had taken an early lead in 19 minutes through Stephen Crawford and at that point they were probably the better side, but Celtic gradually took control and although David Narey was head and shoulders above the rest, he marshalled the defence and calmed his team-mates when the pressure was on, and could do nothing to stop Andy Walker equalising in the 32nd minute.

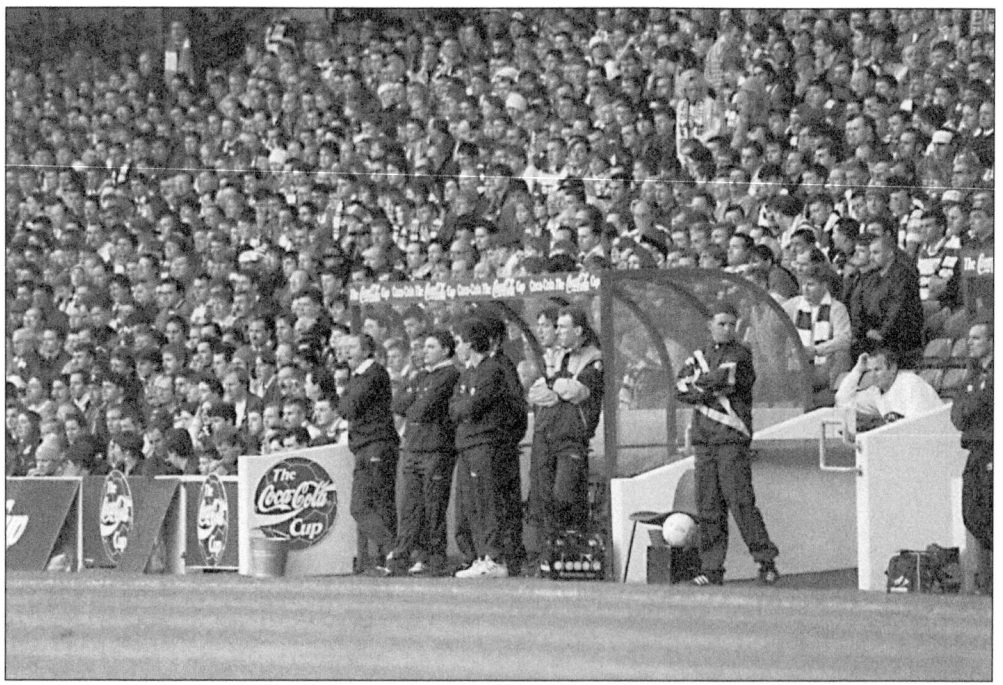

The Rovers bench seemed very laid back considering the tension and the atmosphere.

Scott Thomson in the Raith goal was having a great game, but he couldn't have known what fate was about to hand him.

Into the second half and with the Kirkcaldy fans working as hard as the team, Jason Dair and Stephen Crawford did their best to take some of the pressure off the Raith defence.

Celtic looked to be growing in stature as the second half progressed. It seemed as if Raith would hold out for extra time, but when Andy Walker hit the post and Charlie Nicholas netted the rebound it looked all over for the boys in blue. I remember at that point thinking, as long as we're not embarrassed by a goal landslide. Oh ye of little faith! As the seconds ticked down to the final whistle, Davy Sinclair passed to Jason Dair on the right, Jason jinked passed a Celtic player before firing in a shot between two Celtic defenders. Gordon Marshall in the Celtic goal seemed to have the shot covered, but the ball popped up out of his grasp and there was Gordon Dalziel perfectly placed to head home the equaliser.

The noise from the Govan stand was unbelievable. I managed to fire off a shot of Gordon as he ran to celebrate his goal and then I joined in the celebrations. OK, I'm the club's photographer and I've got a job to do, but underneath it all I'm as big a Rovers fan as you are likely to get and we had just equalised against one of the biggest teams in the country in a cup final.

2-2 and so to extra time.

Celtic fans might argue the point, but Raith looked to be the stronger, more composed side in extra time. Just before referee Jim McCluskey blew the whistle for the end of the extra thirty minutes, Stephen McAnespie had to concede a corner. With the Raith fans' fingernails bitten down to the elbow, Mike Galloway's header from the corner missed the near post by inches.

The penalties were nothing new to the Raith players, as they had had plenty of practice in the semi-final against Airdrie. Luckily for me, Mr McCluskey was kind enough to indicate that the penalties would be taken at my end of the pitch. At 5-5, it was Jason Rowbotham's chance to put Raith 6-5 ahead, and his expertly struck penalty gave Gordon Marshall no chance. Up stepped the Celtic captain Paul McStay. In his television commentary, Jock Brown's words at this point were 'Unthinkable surely for the skipper to miss'. But as McStay walked up to place the ball on the spot, his legs looked like jelly. When he struck the ball, he immediately realised that Scott Thomson had guessed correctly and his spot kick was saved by the Raith goalkeeper. The unthinkable had happened – Raith Rovers had won the Coca-Cola Cup.

As I packed away my camera equipment ready to rush around to the half-way line to photograph the cup presentation, the only thing that went through my mind wasn't that we had just won the cup but that we would be playing in Europe next season. The Govan Stand was alive with jubilant Raith fans, and for once the dream had come true. In a cup final that had enthralled millions throughout Scotland on the television and radio, it was the Raith captain, Gordon Dalziel, who was about to lift the cup.

Something very special had happened in Scottish football, the wee team from the lower league had triumphed. The grins on the faces of the players say it all.

With David Narey clutching his man of the match award, the team waited for the backroom boys to take their place for the photograph of the winners.

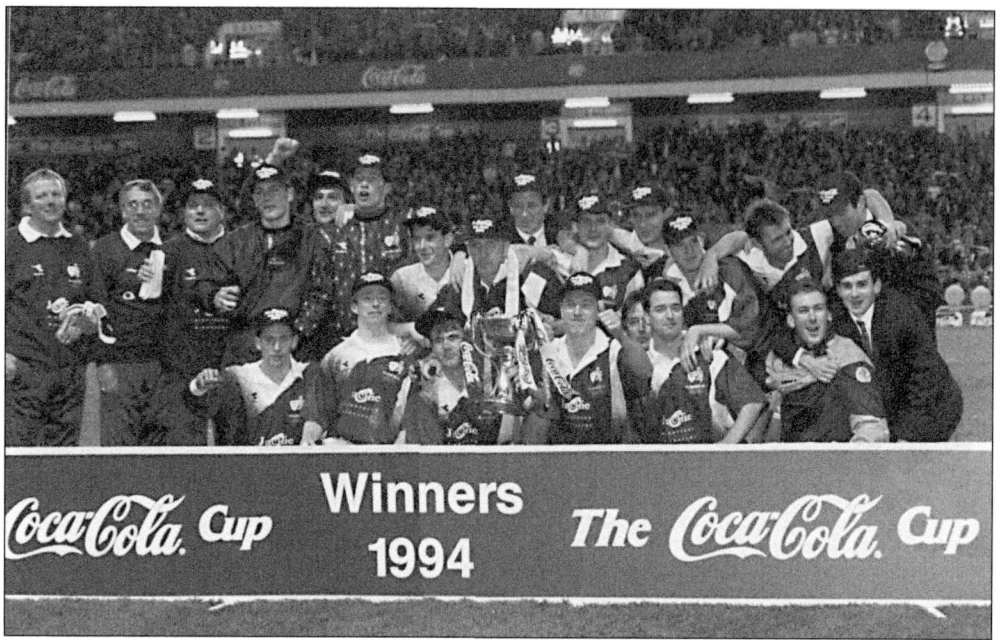

The banner says it all: Raith had won the Coca-Cola Cup!

There was something very special about this cup win. When Raith won promotion to the Premier Division, it was a fantastic feeling. This year, things seemed different, perhaps because of the way that victory came after only five matches, rather than over a season – it seemed all the sweeter. Once back home, and while the rest of the population of Kirkcaldy partied the night away, I sat down on my own in front of the television and watched a video recording of the game from start to finish. When it came to Paul McStay's penalty, I still wasn't sure that Scott Thomson was going to make the save!

Eight

Make Mine a Double

The Saturday after the cup final and it was back to league business with a trip to Ayr and a 1-1 draw. The next day the side were presented with the 'Team of the Year' trophy at the BBC Scotland Sportscene Review of the Year. Then it was back to Starks Park to fight for league points and promotion. St Mirren were Raith's oponents and they did all they could to ruin the party atmosphere as Gordon Dalziel paraded the cup around Starks Park. The programme editor, Paul Gilfillan, described St Mirren as hungrier and faster than the home side and Raith were lucky to scrape a 1-1 draw. If Raith were to make it back to the top division, the side would have to pull their socks up and start picking up win bonuses and – more importantly – points.

The match sponsor for the St Mirren game was United Distillers and they didn't need much persuading to pose for the group photo with the cup. After the photograph was taken and while the guests were admiring the old trophy, I overheard one of them say 'make mine a double'. Was this an instruction to the barman or someone's hopes for the rest of the season? Winning the cup was a fantastic achievement, but to win the cup and league double would surely make the rest of the footballing world sit up and take notice.

Raith Rovers were given a civic reception by the district council and it seemed as though half of the population of Kirkcaldy had turned up to see Jimmy Nicholl and the team show off the cup. I even spotted councillors who had never visited Starks Park in their lives wearing Raith scarves. It's amazing what a little success can do …

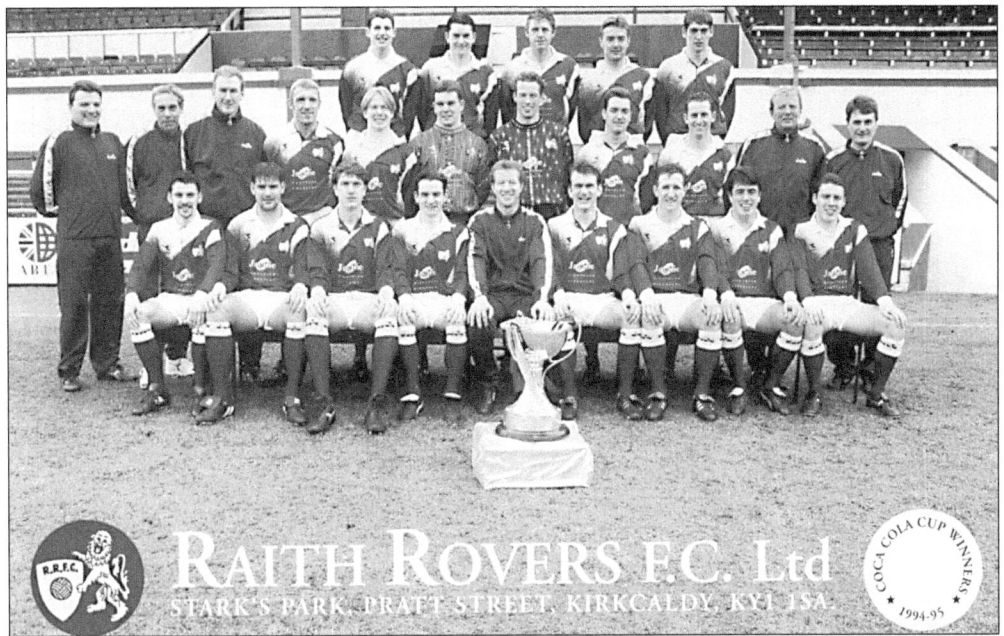

Due to team and player commitments, it took me until February 1995 to arrange the photocall for the official cup-winning team photograph. This copy was made into an envelope with the cup winners' autographs on the back.

By late December, Rovers were sitting fourth in the league and with three points for a win, they had leaders Dundee firmly in their sights. A superb run of victories during January had the cup winners in equal second place with near neighbours Dunfermline and they were only six points off the number one spot. Even Davy Sinclair managed to get his name on the score sheet in the 2-0 win over Hamilton Accies.

Old boy Jock McStay tried his best, but he couldn't prevent Raith from winning 1-0 against his new team Clydebank. In this photograph, Jock is seen holding off Stephen McAnespie. The Raith full back had made number two shirt his own and he was starting to attract the attention of several clubs both north and south of the border.

Although the cup win had come and gone, the memories linger on and one that is particularly fresh in quite a few fans' minds was the fifty-foot club flag that had dominated the Govan Stand that glorious November day. Phil Nicholson, Douglas Campbell, Ewan Gillies, Tony and Gary Oliver and John Greer were the fans behind the giant banner (or in front of it in this photograph).

The Scottish Cup and a league fixture threw up back-to-back meetings with Ayr United at home. The first fixture in the third round of the cup produced a 1-0 win for Raith, with Stephen Crawford scoring the only goal of the game.

More importantly that result was followed seven days later with a 2-1 win for the home side, in the league.

It happened again, following the double-header with Ayr. The Rovers team were paired with Dundee in the fourth round of the Scottish Cup at Dens, then the following week at Starks Park in the league. Raith won the cup game 2-1, but could only manage a 0-0 draw at home. Then it was the turn of Airdrie. Saturday 4 March saw us taking the trip to Broadwood (Aidrie's temporary home). Ally Graham and Jason Dair saw the side through with a goal each in the 2-1 win. Then the 'Diamonds' travelled through to Fife to take us on in the quarter-finals of the cup. Some years after this match, Airdrie's Kenny Black told me that he had never known a team so fired up for a game as Airdrie were and it showed on the park and in front of the television cameras as Kenny's team took Raith apart, winning 4-1. Every Airdrie player played out of his skin, especially the veteran goalkeeper John Martin.

If Raith Rovers needed a boost after the cup defeat, it came in the shape of Tony Rougier. After what seemed to be a marathon of work permit problems, Tony finally entered the fray against Stranraer, but another 1-1 draw saw Raith drop valuable home points. As they went into this game, the home side were equal top of the division on 51 points but third on goal difference behind Dundee and league leaders Dunfermline; the visitors were in last place.

For Raith Rovers fans who wanted an extra special reminder of their club's finest hour, a poster commemorating the Coca-Cola Cup victory was produced from a painting by local artist Liz Foulis. The original painting hangs in the Starks Park boardroom on permanent display.

Two goals from Mickey Cameron to St Mirren's one kept Raith on course for a majestic double.

The last five weeks of the league campaign were nerve-wracking to say the least. Scottish Cup finalists Airdrie dented Raith's promotion hopes with a hard fought 1-0 victory, but Jimmy Nicholl got the team back on the rails with two magnificent away wins against Dundee (2-0) and St. Johnstone (2-1). Stephen Crawford scored a goal in both games and caught the eye of the league sponsor; he was named the Bell's Player of the Month for April.

The final home league fixture of the season was a derby tussle against second-placed Dunfermline, who were only three points behind Raith but had a better goal difference. The stage was set for Raith to win promotion and climb back to the Premier Division in only one season, as long as the visiting side didn't win ... No matter how hard the Raith players tried, they were not able to overcome a determined 'Pars' side. Even when it looked like Gordon Dalziel couldn't miss from point blank range, Guido Van De Kamp managed to pull off an amazing save and the game ended 0-0. At Firhill, the temporary home of Hamilton Accies, Raith only had to draw to win promotion. The game was another tense affair and the final whistle couldn't come fast enough as the two teams slogged out a 0-0 draw. That point was ours, promotion was in the bag in one season. Raith had won the double. The Coca-Cola Cup and the First Division League Championship belonged to us.

Nine

A European Goal

The 1995/96 team photograph. From left to right, back row: D. Sinclair, S. Crawford, R. Raeside, L. Fridge, S. Thomson, B. Potter, J. Broddle, D. Lennon, C. Cameron. Middle row: G. Docherty (physio.), J. Valente (kit man), J. McInally, M. Buist, S. McAnespie, D. Kirkwood, A. Taylor, J. Dair, G. Forrest, G. Robertson, C. McKinlay, M. Quinn, J. Thomson (youth coach), D. Smith (youth coach). Front row: I. McMillan, T. Rougier, S. Dennis, M. Harvey (assistant manager), A. Penman (chairman), J. Nicholl (manager), R. Coyle, B. Wilson, A. Graham. (Photograph: Barry Fimister.)

With Gordon Dalziel transfered to Ayr United, the team was strengthened for the Premier Division campaign with the signing of, from left to right: Alex Taylor, Les Fridge and Jim McInally. Supervising the signing of the contracts are Alex Penman (left) and Willie Gray.

Les Fridge (left) and Scott Thomson (right) would be vying for the number one shirt

Raith's new groundsman, Scott Paterson, had the pitch in perfect condition for the club's first sortie into European competition.

8 August 1995 goes down in club history as the first time Raith Rovers had played a competitive game against European opposition. On a very sunny evening, mascot John Gray led Raith Rovers and Gotu Itrottarfelag of the Faeroe Islands out onto the Starks Park pitch.

Jason Dair (11) had the honour of scoring Raith's first ever competitive European goal.

It looks as if Stephen Crawford has made it onto the score sheet, but this effort came back off the woodwork. Tony Rougier, Stephen McAnespie and Mickey Cameron completed the scoring for Raith in the 4-0 win. On the away trip, Rovers managed a 2-2 draw to go into the first round proper.

The photographers were out in force to capture Raith's first venture onto the European stage.

Before the Coca-Cola Cup game with Arbroath, chairman Alex Penman receives the 1994/95 First Division championship flag from league sponsors Bell's.

Well, we've had the 'windae hingers' but what about these 'pot sitters'?

The 'pot sitters' were making sure of a good vantage point for the visit of Celtic. The team from Glasgow went home with the three points, winning 1-0 despite the efforts of Ally Graham. Five days later, Raith travelled to Parkhead for the third round of the Coca-Cola Cup, but there was to be no repeat of the heroic cup final score of the previous year, Rovers losing 2-1 after extra time.

On 9 September at Ibrox, Rangers ran out winners 0-4, but confidence was still high when Raith had their second taste of European football at Starks Park. This time, the visitors were Akranes of Iceland. Lucky mascot for the game was Ben Clark, who lined up with the team captains and the officials.

The players that took the field that night were, from left to right, back row: Ronnie Coyle, Jason Dair, Shaun Dennis, Scott Thomson, Tony Rougie, Davy Sinclair, Ally Graham, Les Fridge. Front row: David Kirkwood, Barry Wilson, Stephen McAnespie, Ben Clark (mascot), Stephen Crawford, Danny Lennon, Colin Cameron, Julian Broddle.

On a dull night, Danny Lennon opened the scoring by beating Thordur Thorarson in the Akranes goal. The final score was 3-1, but Raith had to fight back from a 1-1 half-time score to take a two-goal lead to Iceland.

Raith were starting to find their feet in the Premier Division and after a comfortable 2-0 win against Kilmarnock, the home side played host to Partick Thistle. Jason Dair turns away as he strikes the ball past Nicky Walker in the 'Jags' goal. Colin Cameron added another two to record a second win in a row (three if you count the Akranes game).

After the trip to Iceland (200 brave fans also made the trip) and the 0-1 defeat, Jimmy Nicholl admitted that he had purposely played with a defensive formation. 'The result was all that mattered,' said Jimmy and he was right because out of the hat (glass bowl, or some other ornamental pot) came the giants of European football, Bayern Munich. What a draw for the wee team from Kirkcaldy. (Or, as they said in Germany, who and where?) Then the realisation came home to the team that it was pointless to play the big guns if they couldn't beat the teams in the home league. The Raith players pulled up their socks and duly demolished Hibs by 3-0, their biggest winning margin since joining the Premier Division. Two goals from Colin Cameron and one from Davy Sinclair helped to put Raith in a safer league position.

The queues were long and winding as the Rovers fans waited patiently for those all-important Bayern Munich tickets.

The programme from the Bayern Munich match.

Starks Park had a 5,000 crowd restriction imposed on it for European games and with the demand for tickets expected to outstrip the normal ground, the club directors had no choice but to switch the game to a more suitable venue. Hibs' Easter Road stadium was chosen for the first leg of the UEFA Cup second round tie. It seemed rather strange when mascot Lewis Alexander led the teams on to the pitch for the 6 p.m. kick-off. It seemed as though both teams were playing away from home and Raith had lost the home advantage.

Within sixteen minutes, Raith had fallen behind to a Jurgen Klinsmann goal, but the boys in blue fought back well, with Jason Dair causing Bayern problems down the wings.

The subs warmed up hoping to get some of the action.

The Kirkcaldy side were coming more into the game and Bayern had to thank their world class 'keeper Oliver Kahn for keeping them in front.

Colin Cameron managed a net-bound shot, but the German 'keeper brilliantly turned his effort over the bar.

Manager Nicholl tried everything he knew to get his team back into the game and brought on Tony Rougier and Stephen Crawford. However, Jurgen Klinsmann put the game beyond Raith with a second goal. Raith Rovers had been beaten at 'home', but the Raith fans in the near 13,000 crowd felt far from embarrassed or let down by their team. Oh! if only we could have played them at Starks Park and really had home advantage.

A 1-0 defeat at the hands of Falkirk dented Raith's league campaign but, typical of Jimmy Nicholl's side, Rovers bounced back with a 2-2 draw against Rangers. Danny Lennon opened the scoring for the home side.

Julian Broddle impressed with his industrious and skilful display against the league leaders.

After an unforgettable trip to Munich which saw Raith give Bayern a fright, with Rovers leading 1-0 at half time, before finally losing 4-1 on aggregate, it was back to league business. An away game at Kilmarnock which ended in a 1-5 defeat was followed by a creditable 0-0 draw against Celtic at Parkhead. This was followed by another goalless draw at home to Motherwell, the 'dour' game matching the 'dreich' weather.

It was unbelievable to think that nearly a year had passed since that unforgettable day at Ibrox when Gordon Dalziel lifted the cup for the 'wee team frae the Lang Toun', but it had to go back. A different colour of ribbons would soon be tied to the three handles of the old trophy, but before it was packed into its very own travelling box, I took the opportunity to photograph the chairman and the members of the board with cup. From left to right: Willie Gray, John Urquhart (president), Alex Penman (chairman), William Shedden, Charles Cant.

If Aberdeen thought they only had to go through the motions against a Raith side which had been knocked out of Europe, suffered in the league and were about to hand back the Coca-Cola Cup, they were badly mistaken. Raith turned on one of their best performances since that night in Munich. Here, Ally Graham is floored by John Inglis in the penalty box.

Up stepped Danny Lennon to send Michael Watt the wrong way. The game may have ended 1-0, but the scoreline did not reflect the home side's superiority on the day. Eight days later, Aberdeen won the Coca-Cola Cup, beating Dundee at Hampden Park; the ribbons on the cup were now red and white.

Ten

Goodbye Jimmy

In the New Year, we welcomed first-footers Kilmarnock. Raith were sitting fifth in the table, two places above and seven points clear of our Ayrshire visitors, and Rovers had a game in hand. Both teams set out to take all three points on offer. Danny Lennon had opened the scoring with an amazing free kick, whipping the ball straight into the net from almost next to the corner flag (a goal worth the admission money on its own). With only three minutes of normal time left, Shaun Dennis punched a Tom Hendry header over the bar. Tom Black scored from the spot to give Killie a share of the points, but referee Stuart Black sent off new signing Mark Humphries in a bad case of mistaken identity.

The Tennents Scottish Cup gave Raith some respite from the rigours of the league campaign, when Queens Park arrived at Starks Park for a third-round tie. This was one of the few cup matches to survive the weather and was played in sometimes blizzard-like conditions. Stephen Crawford was the home side's hero with two goals, Danny Lennon scoring Raith's third.

Appropriately, Les Fridge played in goal against the amateur team from Glasgow and the following week at Tynecastle against Hearts, with the home side winning by two goals to nil. Les had actually managed to save a penalty, John Robertson's spot kick being pushed away by the likeable 'keeper, only for Ronnie Coyle's clearance to bounce off the striker and into the Raith goal.

Before Raith's next home game against Hibernian, the news broke that Jimmy Nicholl and assistant manager Martin Harvey had left to take over the reins at Millwall. Such a move was almost inevitable after all the success that Jimmy had brought to the club and he was linked to nearly all the managerial vacancies that regularly popped up in football circles. This time, though, the offer and the challenge were too good to miss. Jimmy had taken over from Frank Connor in November 1990, his first managerial role in football. His first full season in charge coincided with Raith going full time and with some shrewd signings in the shape of Craig Brewster and Peter Hetherston. Along with the likes of established players Gordon Dalziel and Jock McStay, the youngsters that were coming through and the arrival of Martin Harvey as his assistant, things were looking good for the team and their fans. Raith didn't quite make the grade that first season, but the signs were there and all the hopes and dreams of the fans were realised in season 1992/93 when the Kirkcaldy side won promotion to the Premier Division for the first time. The 1993/94 season was a bit of a let down, with too many draws and not enough wins leading to the inevitable drop back to Division One. Very few, if any, Raith fans could have predicted the outcome of the 1994/95 season: the double. Winning the double or the treble was looked on as the reserve of the two Glasgow giants, with occasionally the new firm having a look in. Some fans and pundits would say that a double or treble only counts if it is won in the top division. But to win your league and a major trophy (and to qualify for Europe) is a double in my book and probably harder than if you're the best team in the top league. Then on to this 1995/96 season – Jimmy again led his charges in the Premier Division and on to those distant fields of Europe. Raith were holding their own in the top league and had acquitted themselves well on the European stage but after Munich, maybe the time was right for a change for both manager and club.

With heavy hearts, the fans thank the man who had given Raith the club's finest hour.

Bobby Geddes made his home debut in goal as Raith welcomed Hibs to Kirkcaldy. The Edinburgh side were one position above Raith in the league, but four points separated the teams. Youth coach Jimmy Thomson prepared the team for the visit of Hibs and he did a good job. Bobby Geddes was outstanding in goal even after a dangerous fall when he collided with one of his own defenders. Davie Kirkwood scored the only goal of the game.

Youth coach Jimmy Thomson and Jim McInally were eventually given the manager and assistant managers job full-time, and they set about strengthening the side, with Steve Kirk arriving at Starks Park along with Peter Duffield, utility player Scott Thomson and Greig McCulloch. Ally Graham moved to Falkirk and Ronnie Coyle, Julian Broddle and Brian Potter were all given free transfers.

Knocked out of the Scottish Cup 2-0 away to Celtic, Jimmy Thomson and Jim Mcinally set about strengthening the Rovers' league position with a superb 3-0 away win at Firhill against bottom-of-the-league Partick. When Aberdeen made the trip to Kirkcaldy, they were looking for a win to consolidate their third place in the league behind Celtic and leaders Rangers. Raith twice took the lead, Stevie Kirk marking his home debut with a goal, and Colin Cameron scored the home side's second, finishing off a brilliant move between new boys Peter Duffield and former Don Scott Thomson. Joe Miller and Jamie Buchan scored for the visitors in the 2-2 draw.

What a happy smiling group we had for the mascots photograph when league leaders Rangers visited. From left to right, back row: Stuart McColl, Willie Young, Danny Lennon. Front row: Scott Ford and his younger sister, Lauren.

The League leaders were in no mood to give up their stranglehold on the title and although Raith put up a brave fight, they couldn't match their multi-million pound opponents. Peter Duffield scored a magnificent opener for the home side and a penalty from Davie Kirkwood had put Raith 2-1 up, but Rangers kept on coming at the Rovers defence and eventually went on to win 4-2.

By the time Hearts came over the Forth to Starks Park, local lad Colin Cameron had joined the 'Jam Tarts' and Miodrag Krivokapic had joined us from Motherwell. Hearts were looking forward to facing Rangers in the Scottish Cup Final and I suppose the Raith fans thought that the visitors' minds might be on other things. Unfortunately, they weren't and Hearts ran out worthy winners 3-1, our only goal coming from a Danny Lennon penalty after Pointon had fouled Peter Duffield inside the box. If you look closely at the photograph, you'll see that the redevelopment programme was already under way, with north end terracing flattened.

Raith Rovers were safe in the Premier Division for at least another season and they celebrated the fact in the traditional way by bringing out a new strip in Raith Rovers tartan, modelled very professionally here by Greig McCulloch.

The last game of the season was meaningless. Raith were safe, as were third bottom Motherwell, but there is always pride at stake, and Raith completed their home fixtures with a comfortable 2-0 win, the goals coming from Scott Thomson and Peter Duffield. The match was notable for the standing ovation that the Motherwell fans gave Miodrag Krivokapic before the start of the match.

The sponsor for the last home game were the 'Neeburs of Geordie Munro', a fine body of men. Their attempts to lift a part of the pitch as a souvenir (after the match of course) were made that much more difficult as there was hardly any grass left on the heavily sanded pitch; there was no point spending money on the playing surface as the Starks Park pitch was about to be levelled. So ended my first five seasons as club photographer and what a five years it had been. Raith Rovers had won promotion to the Premier Division twice, been relegated once, lifted a major trophy for the first time in the club's long history and played in Europe against one of the biggest clubs in the world. The man who had been the architect of the club's success had left and who could guess what the next five years would bring? We would just have to wait and see …